The Holy Spirit

School Age Curriculum

Written by Sarah Hanks
Cover art by Elisabeth Sipe

The Holy Spirit was given as a gift from the Father. This curriculum explores the third person of the Trinity and how He leads, strengthens, teaches, and fills His people. Using passages from mostly the New Testament, children will come to see that the same Holy Spirit who showed up in a powerful way for the apostles lives inside of believers today and how they can have a relationship with Him.

THE HOLY SPIRIT SCHOOL AGE CURRICULUM is the third part in a four-part series that includes I AM SCHOOL AGE CURRICULUM, THE FATHER SCHOOL AGE CURRICULUM, THE HOLY SPIRIT SCHOOL AGE CURRICULUM, and THE TRINITY SCHOOL AGE CURRICULUM. Whether you use the set together or use THE HOLY SPIRIT alone, we pray the children you work with will increase in the knowledge of God.

With interactive lessons and corresponding Family Connection sheets, THE HOLY SPIRIT can be used in a classroom situation as well as a family devotional.

School Age Curriculum

The Holy Spirit

1- Week One –The Holy Spirit Then and Now – 1 Samuel 16:13-14
2- Week Two –The Holy Spirit Leads – Luke 2:22-35
3- Week Three –The Holy Spirit Strengthens – Luke 4:1-14
4- Week Four –The Holy Spirit Teaches – Luke 12:11-12
5- Week Five –The Holy Spirit Reminds – John 14:25-28
6- Week Six –The Holy Spirit Fills – Acts 2:1-13
7- Week Seven- The Holy Spirit Speaks – Acts 8:26-40
8- Week Eight- The Holy Spirit Can't Be Bought – Acts 8:9-24
9- Week Nine- The Holy Spirit is for All – Acts 10:44-48
10- Week Ten –The Holy Spirit Directs – Acts 16:6-10
11- Week Eleven –The Holy Spirit Dwells in Us! – 1 Cor. 6:19

Week One

The Holy Spirit Then and Now

1 Samuel 16:13-14

"And I will pray the Father, and He will give you another Helper, that He may abide with you forever— the Spirit of truth, whom the world cannot receive, because it neither sees Him nor knows Him; but you know Him, for He dwells with you and will be in you. I will not leave you orphans; I will come to you."

John 14:16-18

I. Introduction
   a. This curriculum session, we're going to be learning about the Holy Spirit. Who is the Holy Spirit? What is He like? What does He do? We will explore those questions over the next eleven weeks.
   b. Remember, there is one God in three persons: Father, Son and Holy Spirit.
   c. The Holy Spirit is a person. That doesn't mean He has a human body like we have. A human body is not what makes Him a person. It means He has thoughts and feelings. He speaks and listens.
   d. Some people call the Holy Spirit the Holy Ghost. That's just another translation for spirit that is used in some Bible translations. It doesn't mean that the Holy Spirit is a spooky, white, wispy figure that floats around at night scaring people. Holy Ghost is just another way of saying Holy Spirit.
   e. The Holy Spirit is fully God. He is just as much God as Jesus is God. He is just as much God as God the Father is God.
   f. The Holy Spirit has always been alive. God did not create the Holy Spirit. He has always existed. (We talk more about this in the curriculum The Trinity.)
   g. Today, we are going to learn about the Holy Spirit in the Old Testament and the Holy Spirit in the New Testament.

II. Yesterday, Today, Forever
   a. Hebrews 13:8- Jesus Christ is the same yesterday and today and forever.
   b. If Jesus is the same yesterday, today, and forever, and Jesus, the Father and the Holy Spirit are one, we know that the Holy Spirit doesn't change either. His nature doesn't change. His character doesn't change.
   c. The Holy Spirit is who He is. We don't have to worry that He was nice, but He's suddenly going to turn mean.
   d. However, how the Holy Spirit interacted with human beings did change. Before Jesus was born, He came upon people, but He didn't live inside of them. He helped people, but He didn't stay inside of them forever.
   e. Same Holy Spirit. Different way of interacting.

III. David and Saul

a. King Saul was Israel's first king. He was the king the people chose for themselves because they wanted to be like all the other nations. Things with Saul didn't start out bad. In fact, God's blessing was on Saul as he was anointed king.
b. In 1 Samuel 10, the prophet Samuel told Saul how things were going to play out. He told Saul that he would meet a group of prophets who would be playing instruments and prophesying and then the Spirit of the Lord (The Holy Spirit) would come upon Saul and that Saul would prophesy with them and be turned into another man. Everything happened just as Samuel said it would.
    i. 1 Samuel 10:10- then the Spirit of God came upon him, and he prophesied among them.
c. As time went on, however, Saul stopped trusting in God and began to trust in Himself. When Saul rejected God, God decided that He didn't want Saul to be king anymore.
    i. 1 Samuel 15:23- Because you have rejected the word of the LORD, He also has rejected you from being king.
d. In The Father curriculum, we learned about how Samuel anointed David as king. That happens here in the story. Samuel mourned for Saul until God told him to go and anoint a new king. Samuel went to Jesse's house and looked at his older, strong and handsome sons, but God said no to each one. Then Samuel asked if there were any more sons. Jesse admitted that his youngest, David, was in the field with the sheep. Samuel told him to get him. When David came in, God said "This is the one". Samuel anointed David to be the next king.
e. 1 Samuel 16:13- So Samuel took the horn of oil and anointed him in the presence of his brothers, and from that day on the Spirit of the LORD came powerfully upon David.
f. Here we see that same language we saw with Saul in the beginning. The Holy Spirit "came upon" Saul in the beginning, and here it says that the Holy Spirit "came upon" David powerfully.
g. In the next verse, we see what happened to Saul when He rejected God.
h. 1 Samuel 16:14- Now the Spirit of the LORD had departed from Saul
i. The Holy Spirit had come upon Saul in the beginning, but when Saul decided He didn't want to follow God's ways, the Holy Spirit departed from him, or left him.
j. This wasn't because the Holy Spirit was being mean. The Holy Spirit wants to be where He is welcome and wanted. Saul made him unwelcome when he rejected God's ways.

IV. Then and Now
a. Saul and David are just two examples of many times in the Old Testament when the Holy Spirit came upon people. When the Holy Spirit came upon someone, they had access to His anointing, His power, and His wisdom. The Holy Spirit would often come upon

leaders such as the judges when they needed to fight battles against the enemy. The Holy Spirit gave courage and might.

b. However, the Holy Spirit didn't remain on people forever, and He didn't live in people. Not until Jesus made a way.
c. When Jesus came and died on the cross for our sins and rose again, He made a way for us to go to heaven, yes. But He did more than that. He made a way for God to be inside human beings. The sin that was a barrier before is no longer an issue because Jesus took it on Himself. Now, the Holy Spirit can live on the inside of His creation.
d. Now, when we choose to believe in and follow Jesus, when we give our lives to Him, the Holy Spirit comes and makes His home inside of us. He is with us all the time! He never leaves us.
e. We will talk more about this at the end of this curriculum session, but for the next week, each morning when you wake up, try to remember that you have God on the inside of you. Acknowledge Him with a "Good morning, Holy Spirit. Thank You for living inside me today."
f. He is with us all the time. The more we recognize that He's there, the more we will get to know Him.

Week Two

The Holy Spirit Leads

Luke 2:22-35

"But God has revealed them to us through His Spirit. For the Spirit searches all things, yes, the deep things of God. For what man knows the things of a man except the spirit of the man which is in him? Even so no one knows the things of God except the Spirit of God." 1 Corinthians 2:10-11

I. Review
   a. For the next ten weeks, we're going to be learning about The Holy Spirit. We will be exploring who He is, what He's like, and what He does.
   b. Last week we learned that although the Holy Spirit doesn't change, how He interacted with human beings in the Old Testament was different than how He interacts with believers today. How so?
   c. Today we're going to learn how the Holy Spirit leads us.

II. The Holy Spirit Leads Simeon
   a. When Jesus was just a baby, Joseph and Mary brought him to the temple to dedicate him to God. It was kind of like what a baby dedication is today.
   b. An old man named Simeon was at the temple.
   c. Luke 2:25- Now there was a man in Jerusalem called Simeon, who was righteous and devout. He was waiting for the consolation of Israel, and the Holy Spirit was on him.
   d. Simeon had a heart posture of watching and waiting. He was watching and waiting for the Messiah, for the One who would console, or comfort, Israel. His people were being oppressed by Rome and he was on the lookout for the Savior who would make the wrong things right.
   e. The Bible says that the Holy Spirit was *upon* Simeon. Remember, since Jesus hadn't died and gone back up to Heaven yet, the Holy Spirit didn't live inside of people yet.
   f. Luke 2:26- It had been revealed to him by the Holy Spirit that he would not die before he had seen the Lord's Messiah.
   g. So, the Holy Spirit showed him that his watching and waiting wouldn't be for nothing. He was going to see the Messiah with his own eyes.
   h. Luke 2:27-28- **27** Moved by the Spirit, he went into the temple courts. When the parents brought in the child Jesus to do for him what the custom of the Law required, **28** Simeon took him in his arms and praised God…
   i. The Holy Spirit told Simeon to go to the temple courts at just the right time.
   j. When he saw the baby Jesus, he knew that this baby was the Messiah. How? Because the Holy Spirit revealed it to him.
   k. He took the baby Jesus into his arms and blessed him. Then he prophesied to Joseph and Mary and blessed them as well.
   l. Luke 2:29-35- "Sovereign Lord, as you have promised,

      you may now dismiss[c] your servant in peace.

30 For my eyes have seen your salvation,

31 which you have prepared in the sight of all nations:

32 a light for revelation to the Gentiles,

and the glory of your people Israel."

33 The child's father and mother marveled at what was said about
him.34 Then Simeon blessed them and said to Mary, his mother: "This
child is destined to cause the falling and rising of many in Israel, and
to be a sign that will be spoken against, 35 so that the thoughts of many
hearts will be revealed. And a sword will pierce your own soul too."

III. Revealing the Holy Spirit

a. How does this true story from God's Word show us who the Holy Spirit is and what He does? We see several things in this passage.
b. The Holy Spirit revealed to Simeon that he would see the Messiah before he died. The Holy Spirit reveals to us the mysteries of God. He lets us in on God's secrets. He shows us what God is thinking about and what God is doing.
c. Secondly, the Holy Spirit led and guided Simeon to the right place at just the right time. The Holy Spirit loves to lead us. He wants to guide us as well. His timing is always perfect and He will position us so that we will have the same type of "divine appointments". Some people might think it was just a coincidence. They might say Simeon just happened to be in the temple at the exact same time that Joseph and Mary brought Jesus, but we know that isn't true. This was an act of the Holy Spirit.
d. Thirdly, the Holy Spirit showed Simeon which person in the temple was the Messiah. Think about it. Simeon wouldn't have even known for sure that it would have been a baby. It could have been anyone, and there would have been a lot of people there. How could he find the Messiah in that huge crowd? The Holy Spirit pointed him out.
e. We also saw how Simeon, by the power of the Holy Spirit, prophesied over Jesus and Mary.
f. So how did Simeon know what the Holy Spirit was saying? The Bible doesn't tell us how the Holy Spirit spoke to Simeon. All we know is that Simeon was watching and waiting. Simeon positioned his heart to listen and pay attention.
g. If we will pay attention, we can learn to be led by the Holy Spirit too. The Holy Spirit hasn't changed. He has always led God's people. He still leads God's people today. He wants to lead you.
h. Learning how to listen for the Holy Spirit's voice may take time. Remember that Simeon was an old man. He probably had a lot of practice. We need practice too, but you don't have to wait until you're old to be led by the Holy Spirit. You can start paying attention to Him today and He will be faithful to lead you.

Week Three

The Holy Spirit Strengthens

Luke 4:1-14

"That He would grant you, according to the riches of his glory to be strengthened with might by His Spirit in the inner man." Ephesians 3:16

I. Review
   a. Over the next couple months, we're going to be getting the know the Holy Spirit better.
   b. We've learned how the Holy Spirit came upon people in the Old Testament, but after Jesus died, rose again, and went back to heaven, the Holy Spirit came to live inside of believers.
   c. Last week we learned how the Holy Spirit led Simeon to be in just the right place at just the right time so that he could meet the Messiah.
   d. Today we're going the learn about how the Holy Spirit strengthens us.

II. Into the Wilderness
   a. Sometimes the Holy Spirit leads us to do things that are neat and fun, but sometimes the He leads us to do things that are important, but not fun.
   b. Luke 4:1-2- Jesus, full of the Holy Spirit, left the Jordan and was led by the Spirit into the wilderness, **2** where for forty days he was tempted by the devil.
   c. This was when Jesus was older and about to start His ministry, right after He was baptized.
   d. It's important to realize that He didn't go into the wilderness because the Holy Spirit left Him. The Holy Spirit didn't abandon Jesus to the devil. Instead, Jesus was full of the Holy Spirit and the Holy Spirit led Him into this show down with the enemy so that He could emerge from the wilderness victorious.
   e. Luke 4:2- He ate nothing during those days, and at the end of them he was hungry.
   f. Jesus fasted for forty days and then devil came to him and tried to get Him to turn His back on God.

III. Using the Sword of the Spirit
   a. Luke 4:3- The devil said to him, "If you are the Son of God, tell this stone to become bread."
   b. Jesus, fully man, was hungry. He hadn't eaten, and His body was weak. The devil came trying to make the best of that weakness by tempting Him to use His power in a way that God hadn't meant for Him to.
   c. Was Jesus the Son of God? Could He have turned the stone into bread? Yes and yes! But Jesus wasn't playing the devil's game.
   d. Luke 4:4- Jesus answered, "It is written: 'Man shall not live on bread alone.'
      i. What is Jesus doing here? He is using the Word of God – Scripture- to fight the enemy. He is quoting Deuteronomy 8:3.
   e. Ephesians 6 talks about the armor of God. Armor is what someone wears when they are doing battle. In this passage, Jesus is doing battle with the

enemy and He is clothed in the armor of God. What piece of the armor is He using when He quotes Deuteronomy 8:3?

f. Ephesians 6:17- Take the helmet of salvation and the *sword of the Spirit*, which is the *word of God.*
g. The sword of the Spirit, the Holy Spirit's sword, is the word of God.
h. Jesus is fighting the devil in partnership with the Holy Spirit.
i. The passage in Ephesians was originally written in the Greek language. The Greek word used in Ephesians 6:17 for "word" in the phrase "word of God" is rhema.
j. There are two main words pertaining to the word of God: logos and rhema. Logos is talking about the whole word of God, or your entire Bible. Rhema is talking about a specific word, a specific statement. It's just the right verse at just the right time.
k. That's what the sword of the Spirit is and what the Holy Spirit gives us: just the right verse at just the right time so that we can defeat the enemy.
l. Luke 4:5-7- The devil led him up to a high place and showed him in an instant all the kingdoms of the world. **6** And he said to him, "I will give you all their authority and splendor; it has been given to me, and I can give it to anyone I want to. **7** If you worship me, it will all be yours."
m. The devil tries again. The Bible says that this world is under the devil's sway until Jesus comes back to rule and reign on the earth. The devil offers Jesus a shortcut. He could be the King of the world NOW instead of later if He would just bow down and worship the devil.
n. What does Jesus do? He uses the sword of the Spirt again.
o. Luke 4:8- Jesus answered, "It is written: 'Worship the Lord your God and serve him only.
    i. Jesus quotes Deuteronomy 6:13.
p. The devil tried to trick Jesus one more time.
q. Luke 4:9-11- The devil led him to Jerusalem and had him stand on the highest point of the temple. "If you are the Son of God," he said, "throw yourself down from here. **10** For it is written:

"'He will command his angels concerning you
  to guard you carefully;
11 they will lift you up in their hands,
  so that you will not strike your foot against a stone.'"

    i. This time the devil tries to quote Scripture to Jesus. He quotes Psalm 91:11-12, but because he is not being led by the Holy Spirit, it is not just the right Scripture at just the right time.
r. Luke 4:12- Jesus answered, "It is said: 'Do not put the Lord your God to the test.'
    i. Jesus comes back with Deuteronomy 6:16.
s. Luke 4:13- Now when the devil had ended every temptation, he departed from Him until an opportune time.

t. This same passage in Matthew says that angels then came to minister to Jesus.
u. Then what happened? Now that the devil left?
v. Luke 4:14- Then Jesus returned in the power of the Spirit to Galilee.

IV. Revealing the Holy Spirit

a. What can we learn about the Holy Spirit from this passage?
b. First of all, we saw once again that the Holy Spirit leads. What He leads us to might be fun and cool, or it might not be, but it is always important.
c. He doesn't lead us somewhere and then abandon us. He is with us, strengthening us in the midst of battle.
d. The Holy Spirit gives us the power and strength to fight the fight of faith.
e. The Holy Spirit strengthened Jesus so that He would not give into temptation.
f. Sometimes the Holy Spirit might lead us to do things that are hard, but He will always help us and give us the strength that we need to follow Him.
g. The sword of the Spirit – the Holy Spirit's weapon – is the rhema of God. It is the right word at the right time. We fight the enemy using the word of God and the Holy Spirit helps us by showing us what Bible verse to use when.

Week Four

The Holy Spirit Teaches

Luke 12:11-12

"For the Holy Spirit will teach you in that very hour what you ought to say." Luke 12:12

I. Review

a. This session we are getting to know the Holy Spirit better.

b. We learned that the Holy Spirit used to come upon certain people, but now that Jesus came, died, was raised, and ascended to the Father, He lives inside all believers.

c. We learned that the Holy Sprit leads us.

d. Last week we learned that the Holy Spirit strengthens us.

e. We also learned that the sword of the Sprit is the word of God. Do you remember what that is called in Greek? The rhema of God. That means a specific word. The right word at the right time. The Holy Spirit gives us the right Scripture at the right time in order to fight the enemy.

f. Today we're going to learn about how the Holy Spirit teaches.

II. Don't Be Afraid

a. When Jesus had His disciples with Him, He told them not to be afraid to tell other people about Him. He said that if they were not afraid to tell people about Jesus, that Jesus would not be afraid to talk about them to the Father.

b. Jesus warned His disciples that one day after Jesus had gone back to Heaven, a lot of people would not like people talking about Jesus. They wouldn't want anyone to tell people about Jesus. They would make rules that no one could talk about Jesus. In those times Jesus did not want His disciples to be afraid.

c. He wanted them to continue to tell people about Jesus so that a lot of people could be saved.

d. Luke 12:11-12- "When you are brought before synagogues, rulers and authorities, do not worry about how you will defend yourselves or what you will say, **12** for the Holy Spirit will teach you at that time what you should say."

e. Jesus was saying that the disciples would be brought before leaders of different kinds. Some of them Jewish leaders who wouldn't believe Jesus was the Messiah. Some of them Gentile leaders who didn't know about Jesus. They would be brought before these leaders as if they had done something wrong by believing in Jesus and telling people about Jesus.

f. Have you ever been accused of doing something wrong when you didn't do it? Have you ever tried to convince someone- maybe your mom or dad, maybe a teacher- that you didn't do anything wrong?

g. Have you ever practiced what you were going to say to someone before you had to say it? Maybe in front of a mirror, maybe out loud to yourself, or maybe just in your head? Have you ever tried to make sure you would sound really smart or cool when the time came when you would get to talk to that person?

h. It is natural to rehearse what we want to say beforehand, especially if we feel like we need to defend ourselves to someone. Jesus knew that this would be the disciples' natural tendency when they were brought before rulers accused of wrongdoing, but He told the disciples not to do it.
i. Instead of worrying about what they were going to say, He told them to trust the Holy Spirit. He promised that the Holy Spirit would teach them what to say when they needed to say it.
j. Think of the best teacher you've ever had in school or at church. What was it about them that made them a great teacher?
k. The Holy Spirit is a teacher, and He's a really, really good one! He teaches us exactly what we need to know exactly when we need to know it. He teaches us the perfect words to speak for the testimony of Jesus to go forth. When we don't know what to say, the Holy Spirit does!

III. Paul before Agrippa

a. There are many examples in the New Testament of the Holy Spirit teaching the apostles what to say right when they needed to say it. One such example is Paul when he was brought before King Agrippa.
b. Paul was being held as a prisoner in Caesarea by Festus. Some Jews wanted to charge Paul with wrongdoing because they didn't like him preaching about Jesus. They couldn't prove the things they were accusing him of.
c. Acts 25:8- In his defense, Paul said by the Holy Spirit, "I have done nothing wrong. I've committed no offense against Jewish law, or against the temple, or against Caesar." (Quotes from this passage in The Passion Version)
d. Festus didn't really understand the charges brought against Paul and asked Paul if he would be willing to go to Jerusalem and be charged there. Paul instead appealed to Ceasar so that he would later be taken to Rome.
e. While Paul was being held in Caesarea, King Agrippa came to visit Festus and wanted to see Paul because he was curious about him.
f. Acts 26:1-3- King Agrippa said to Paul, "You may now state your case." Paul motioned with his hand for silence, then began his defense. **2** "King Agrippa, I consider myself highly favored to stand before you today and answer the charges made against me by the Jews. **3** Because you, more than anyone else, are very familiar with the customs and controversies among the Jewish people, I now ask for your patience as I state my case.
g. Paul talked about how he used to be a Pharisee, strict in the Jewish traditions. He talked about how he used to persecute Christians. He told King Agrippa about his experience on the road to Damascus, how He saw Jesus and how Jesus talked to him.
h. Acts 25:19-21- "So you see, King Agrippa, I have not been disobedient to what was revealed to me from heaven. **20** For it was in Damascus that I first declared the truth. And then I went to Jerusalem and throughout our nation, and even to other nations, telling people everywhere that they must repent and turn to God and demonstrate it with a changed life.[o] **21** That's why the Jews seized me when I was in the temple and tried to murder me.

i. Paul then told them he was saying the same thing to them that he said to everyone: the Jesus had to suffer and die and rise from the dead.
j. Festus interrupted Paul and said that he was crazy!
    i. Acts 26:24- Festus interrupted Paul's defense,[r] blurting out, "You're out of your mind! All this great learning of yours is driving you crazy."
k. Paul said he wasn't crazy and spoke to King Agrippa saying
    i. Acts 26:27- Don't you believe the prophets, King Agrippa? I know that you do."
l. Acts 26:28- Agrippa responded, "In such a short time you are nearly persuading me to become a Christian."
m. This passage illustrates how the Holy Spirit was with Paul and taught Paul what to say when he needed to say it.
n. Just because the Holy Spirit gives people the perfect words from the heart of God doesn't mean that everyone is going to respond with happy hearts. There were a lot of people who didn't like Jesus while He walked on the earth and there will still be people who reject Him and anything having to do with Him today.
o. When Festus heard Paul's words given by the Holy Spirit, he thought they were crazy! But King Agrippa was moved by them. They were the right words at the right time. They weren't Paul's words that Paul recited in front of a mirror to make himself look good. They were the Holy Spirit's words that the Holy Spirit taught Paul.

IV. Conclusion
a. The Holy Spirit is a good teacher. We don't have to be afraid that we won't say everything right or do everything right. We can rest in the fact that He is really good at His job.
b. He will teach us. Are we willing to learn from Him?
c. If we are, He will put God's words in our mouths and we can partner with Him in exciting ways.
d. Jesus loves the Holy Spirit and the Holy Spirit loves Jesus. The Holy Spirit is here to help us tell others about Jesus. He's the Holy Spirit's favorite topic of conversation!

Week Five:

The Holy Spirit Reminds

John 14:25-28, John 2:22

"But the Helper, the Holy Spirit, whom the Father will send in My name, He will teach you all things, and bring to your remembrance all things that I said to you."

John 14:26

I. Review

a. We've been getting to know the Holy Spirit better. So far we've learned that Holy Spirit

i. Leads God's people,

ii. Strengthens God's people, and

iii. Teaches God's people.

b. What's one thing you've learned about the Holy Spirit?

c. Today we're going to learn about how the Holy Spirit reminds.

II. The Helper

a. The Holy Spirit is called the Helper. Why do you think He is called the Helper? What does He help us with?

b. When it got closer and closer to the time Jesus would die, rise again, then ascend to the Father, Jesus started to prepare His disciples for the fact that He would be going away. His disciples had hung out with Him all the time for three years and they were really close to Him. They were really going to miss Him.

c. One main way Jesus prepared His disciples was by telling them about the Holy Spirit who would come and live inside of them shortly after Jesus went back to the Father.

d. One day, Jesus talked to His disciples about the Holy Spirit and what the Holy Spirit would do for them after Jesus wasn't with them anymore.

e. John 14:25-27-These things I have spoken to you while being present with you.**26** But the Helper, the Holy Spirit, whom the Father will send in My name, He will teach you all things, and bring to your remembrance all things that I said to you. **27** Peace I leave with you, My peace I give to you; not as the world gives do I give to you. Let not your heart be troubled, neither let it be afraid.

f. Jesus was saying that at that moment, He could talk to His disciples face to face, but soon He wouldn't be able to. He didn't want His disciples to be troubled – or sad- about that because they would have the Holy Spirit as their Helper.

g. The Holy Spirit would teach them ALL THINGS about Jesus. Isn't that cool? We learned last week that Holy Spirit is a teacher and that He's really good at His job. Here we see Jesus saying that Holy Spirit doesn't just teach us what to say to others about Jesus. He teaches us all things pertaining to Jesus.

h. Jesus also said that the Holy Spirit would bring to their remembrance everything that Jesus said to them. The Holy Spirit would remind them of Jesus words.

i. Have you ever been talking to someone and they had so many interesting things to say that you found it hard to remember everything? Or have you ever been in class and your teacher is teaching new information faster than you can take it all in? You might think "There's no way I can remember all of this!"
j. Think of how the disciples felt! Jesus was teaching them all the time, each and every day for three years. How could they ever remember everything He said?
k. Jesus promised that the Holy Spirit would be their Helper, helping them to remember all that He said to them.

III. Talking about the Temple
a. When Jesus was alive, He cleansed the temple. That doesn't mean that he got out a mop and started cleaning.
b. John 2:14- And He found in the temple those who sold oxen and sheep and doves, and the money changers doing business. [15] When He had made a whip of cords, He drove them all out of the temple, with the sheep and the oxen, and poured out the changers' money and overturned the tables. [16] And He said to those who sold doves, "Take these things away! Do not make My Father's house a house of merchandise!"
c. Jesus was so angry that people were buying and selling things there as a way to make money instead of the temple being a place of prayer that He made quite a scene! He turned tables over, money spilling everywhere, and drove out the people selling those things and their animals with a whip!
d. A lot of the people got mad when He did this and they said, "Tell us who gave you the authority to do these things?"
e. Then Jesus said, "Destroy this temple and I will raise it again in three days."
f. He wasn't talking about the building the temple. He was talking about Himself. After he died, He rose from the dead three days later.
g. When He said this, though, the disciples didn't know what He was talking about.
h. John 2:22- After he was raised from the dead, his disciples recalled what he had said. Then they believed the scripture and the words that Jesus had spoken.
i. After Jesus was raised from the dead, the disciples remembered how Jesus talked about how He would destroy the temple and build it again in three days. Then they understood that He wasn't talking about a building made out of bricks. He was talking about Himself. Jesus' words clicked in their minds and they got it! They understood.
j. Who helped them remember Jesus' words? The Holy Spirit did! And who taught them what Jesus' words really meant? The Holy Spirit did!

IV. Our Helper
a. The Father sent the Holy Spirit to the disciples to help them remember what Jesus said to them while He walked the earth, but the Holy Spirit is also our Helper.

b. When we read the Bible, it's as if those verses go in file folders in the back of our minds, but also in our spirits. When we go through a particular season in our lives or face a certain circumstance and we need God's wisdom, the Holy Spirit helps us by grabbing the Scripture that we need from that file folder and handing it to us, if we are willing to listen to Him.
c. It is that rhema word – that right word at the right time – that we talked about last week.
d. The Holy Spirit helps us by reminding us of what Jesus has already spoken to us in His Word, as well as prophetic words that others have spoken over us in the past or that He has given us directly.
e. Not only that, but the Holy Spirit is there to teach us what those Scriptures mean. He loves to give us revelation about Jesus and His Word.
f. If we want the Holy Spirit to remind us of what Jesus has spoken in His Word, don't you think we should probably read The Word? Reading your Bible and talking with the Holy Spirit about it is a great way to draw closer to Him.
g. While you read passages of Scripture, pause every so often and ask questions. Ask "Holy Spirit, why did Jesus say that? What did He mean? Why did God do it that way? Help me to understand." The Helper loves to help!

Week Six

The Holy Spirit Fills

Acts 2:1-13

"All of them were filled with the Holy Spirit and began to speak in other tongues as the Spirit enabled them." Acts 2:4

I. Review
  a. This curriculum session, we've been getting to know the Holy Spirit better.
  b. We've learned that He lives inside of God's people.
  c. We've learned that He leads us.
  d. We've learned that He strengthens us and helps us fight against the enemy with the Sword of the Spirit, which is the rhema of God.
  e. We've learned that He teaches us what to say. He helps us to tell others about Jesus.
  f. Last week we learned that the Holy Spirit reminds us of Jesus' words and helps us to understand them.
  g. Today we're going to learn about how the Holy Spirit fills us.

II. Pentecost
  a. Remember that when Jesus was telling His disciples that He was going away, back to Heaven, He told them not to worry because after He left, the Father would send the Helper, which is the Holy Spirit.
  b. After Jesus was raised from the dead, He hung out with the disciples for forty days before going back to Heaven to be with the Father. During that time Jesus told the disciples to wait in the city for the Holy Spirit to come.
  c. Luke24:49- I am going to send you what my Father has promised; but stay in the city until you have been clothed with power from on high. (NIV)
  d. What the Father has promised was the Holy Spirit. Jesus told them to stay there until He came. He said that when the Holy Spirit came, it would be like the disciples were putting on clothes of power from Heaven.
  e. The Passion Translation puts it this way: "And I will send the fulfillment of the Father's promise to you. So stay here in the city until the mighty power of heaven falls upon you and wraps around you."
  f. Acts 2:1- When the Day of Pentecost had fully come, they were all with one accord in one place.
  g. The Day of Pentecost meant that this happened during the Jewish festival of Pentecost which was also known as Shavuot or the Feast of Weeks.
  h. The disciples and a group of Jesus' followers were listening to Jesus' instructions. They staid in the city and they were waiting there, praying together.
  i. Acts 2:2- And suddenly there came a sound from heaven, as of a rushing mighty wind, and it filled the whole house where they were sitting.

j. Suddenly everyone HEARD a sound. The sound of a rushing mighty wind filled the house.
k. Acts 2:3- Then there appeared to them divided tongues, as of fire, and *one* sat upon each of them.
l. Then they SAW something that looked like tongues of fire sitting over each of their heads.
m. Acts 2:4a- And they were all filled with the Holy Spirit
n. Then everyone was filled with the Holy Spirit. The third person of the Trinity came inside each person in that house, filling them with the presence of God.
o. Acts 2:4b- and began to speak with other tongues, as the Spirit gave them utterance.
p. The Holy Spirit gave these people different languages to speak in, languages they had never known before. All of the sudden, they could speak fluently in a completely different language that they had never studied.
    i. When we talk about speaking in tongues there are two main types of tongues. This is one type. The disciples were speaking a language that someone else of that nationality could understand. It would be like you suddenly being able to speak Spanish when you never learned how to and the person next to you suddenly being able to speak French never having studied. People from Mexico and people from France would be able to understand what you guys were saying.
    ii. The other type of tongue is more common today and is where you speak in a language that no one understands except for the Holy Spirit and your spirit. Your mind doesn't know what you are saying but your spirit is speaking to God by the power of the Holy Spirit.
    iii. The gift of tongues is a gift of the Holy Spirit and it is a gift we can ask Him for.
q. Acts 2:5-8- And there were dwelling in Jerusalem Jews, devout men, from every nation under heaven. 6 And when this sound occurred, the multitude came together, and were confused, because everyone heard them speak in his own language. 7 Then they were all amazed and marveled, saying to one another, "Look, are not all these who speak Galileans? 8 And how *is it that* we hear, each in our own language in which we were born?
r. The people in the city were shocked to hear these people from Galilee talking in all different kinds of languages. And what were the disciples saying in those tongues?
s. Acts 2:11- "we hear them speaking in our own tongues the wonderful works of God."
t. They were speaking about God! They were telling of Jesus! Of course! The Holy Spirit's favorite topic of conversation.

u. Acts 2:12-13- So they were all amazed and perplexed, saying to one another, "Whatever could this mean?"

[13] Others mocking said, "They are full of new wine."

v. Remember how we said that not everyone loved and will love Jesus and not everyone loved and will love the Holy Spirit either. Some people were amazed, and others made fun of the disciples, saying that they were drunk. Many people make fun of what they don't understand.

III. What happens when we're filled?

a. So, what happens when we are filled with the Holy Spirit? What happened to the disciples when they were filled with the Holy Spirit?
b. Let's look at Peter. What was Peter like before he was filled with the Holy Spirit?
c. Right before Jesus died on the cross, He told His disciples that One of them was going to betray Him. Peter thought that he would be faithful to Jesus no matter what, but Jesus had to break it to him. Peter would deny Him.
d. Matthew 26:33-35- Peter replied, "Even if all fall away on account of you, I never will."

[34] "Truly I tell you," Jesus answered, "this very night, before the rooster crows, you will disown me three times."

[35] But Peter declared, "Even if I have to die with you, I will never disown you." And all the other disciples said the same.

e. Jesus was right, of course. When the soldiers came to arrest Jesus, all of His disciples, including Peter, forsook Him and ran away. Peter ended up following Jesus at a distance.
f. Mark 14:66-72- [66] While Peter was below in the courtyard, one of the servant girls of the high priest came by. [67] When she saw Peter warming himself, she looked closely at him.

"You also were with that Nazarene, Jesus," she said.

[68] But he denied it. "I don't know or understand what you're talking about," he said, and went out into the entryway.[g]

[69] When the servant girl saw him there, she said again to those standing around, "This fellow is one of them." [70] Again he denied it.

After a little while, those standing near said to Peter, "Surely you are one of them, for you are a Galilean."

[71] He began to call down curses, and he swore to them, "I don't know this man you're talking about."

72 Immediately the rooster crowed the second time. Then Peter remembered the word Jesus had spoken to him: "Before the rooster crows twice you will disown me three times." And he broke down and wept.

g. Peter was broken over his weakness. He wanted to be strong and follow Jesus no matter what, but in the end he was afraid and denied knowing his friend. He needed strength. He needed supernatural boldness. Thankfully, God had a plan in place to give Peter exactly what he needed.
h. After Peter was filled with the Holy Spirit, this man who was afraid to even admit that he knew Jesus stood up and told the entire crowd about Jesus. He preached a sermon to the city, calling them to repent, believe in Jesus, and receive the Holy Spirit.
i. Three thousand people were saved and baptized that day because Peter declared the gospel to them. Three thousand!
j. When people are filled with the Holy Spirit they have supernatural power inside of them to do what they couldn't do before. They have courage and boldness.
k. When people are filled with the Holy Spirit they might speak in tongues.
l. When people are filled with the Holy Spirit they might prophesy.
m. When people are filled with the Holy Spirit, they will have the testimony of Jesus on their lips. The Holy Spirit loves to talk about Jesus and so do people who are filled with the Holy Spirit.
n. *Take time to pray for children who want to be filled with the Holy Spirit.

Week Seven

The Holy Spirit Can't Be Bought

Acts 8:9-24

"It is the Spirit who gives life; the flesh profits nothing. The words that I speak to you are spirit, and they are life." John 6:63

I. Review
   a. Name three things you have learned about the Holy Spirit so far.
   b. Today we're going to learn about how someone tried to buy the Holy Spirit. How do you think that turned out?

II. Is the Holy Spirit for sale?
   a. When persecution arose against the church because of Saul of Tarsus (who later became the apostle Paul) the apostles scattered and went different places, preaching about Jesus wherever they went.
      i. Persecution means people were getting in trouble for being Christians. Saul was dragging them off to jail.
   b. Phillip went to Samaria and preached about Jesus there. Do you remember Samaria? The Jews considered the Samaritans their enemies, but Phillip understood that Jesus loved all people and wanted the Samaritans to be saved too.
   c. Acts 8:6-8- When the crowds heard Philip and saw the signs he performed, they all paid close attention to what he said. 7 For with shrieks, impure spirits came out of many, and many who were paralyzed or lame were healed. 8 So there was great joy in that city.
   d. A man named Simon was there and he practiced sorcery. Sorcery is where he could do some powerful things, but he got his power from the devil and not from God. The Bible says that sorcery is a sin and God's people are to stay away from it.
   e. Simon thought he was someone great and so did the people of Samaria. Everyone thought he was this amazing guy because of his sorcery.
   f. But what happened when Simon saw true power? The power of the Holy Spirit?
   g. Acts 8:12-13- But when they believed Philip as he proclaimed the good news of the kingdom of God and the name of Jesus Christ, they were baptized, both men and women. 13 Simon himself believed and was baptized. And he followed Philip everywhere, astonished by the great signs and miracles he saw.
   h. He was blown away! He believed in Jesus and was baptized. Satan's power is nothing compared to God's power!
   i. The apostles heard that Samaria had accepted the Word of God and they sent Peter and John to Samaria to help Phillip and to pray that the Holy Spirit would be poured out there. The Samaritans had been water baptized, but they hadn't yet been baptized with the Holy Spirit (or filled with the Holy Spirit).
   j. So, Peter and John came and put their hands on the people and they received the Holy Spirit.

k. Acts 8:18-19- When Simon saw that the Spirit was given at the laying on of the apostles' hands, he offered them money [19] and said, "Give me also this ability so that everyone on whom I lay my hands may receive the Holy Spirit.

l. Simon thought that he could buy the Holy Spirit! He wanted to give the apostles money in exchange for the ability to lay hands on people and have them receive the Holy Spirit. Does it work like that?

m. Acts 8:20-23- Peter answered: "May your money perish with you, because you thought you could buy the gift of God with money! [21] You have no part or share in this ministry, because your heart is not right before God.[22] Repent of this wickedness and pray to the Lord in the hope that he may forgive you for having such a thought in your heart. [23] For I see that you are full of bitterness and captive to sin."

n. Peter told him to repent of his wickedness. Simon's heart was not right before God. He told Simon to pray to God and ask God to forgive him.

o. The Holy Spirit can't be bought with money. He is a person. He has thoughts and feelings. It is wicked to think that you can buy or sell a person and it is wicked to think you can buy or sell the Holy Spirit.

p. Not only is He a person, He is God. He is Holy. He is the Creator of the Universe and the One who upholds all things. How could a human control Him? Simon didn't understand His holiness.

q. Peter had a word of knowledge for Simon. Peter saw something in the spirit about Simon's heart. He saw that there was bitterness there and that Simon's heart was in chains to his sin. That was a prophetic word given to Simon. Peter didn't know this in the natural. It was revelation given to him by the Holy Spirit.

    i. When he said, "I see", it didn't mean that he could see it on the outside. It meant that the Holy Spirit opened up his spirit eyes so that he could see a picture of Simon's heart.

    ii. Even though Simon believed in Jesus and was baptized, he needed to be set free from bitterness and chains of sin that probably had a lot to do with his history of partnering with Satan in sorcery for many years.

    iii. God can set people free of those things, but Simon needed to repent, or turn away from that way of life and that way of thinking.

III. How do we treat the Holy Spirit?

a. How do we treat the Holy Spirit?

b. Do we treat Him like He is a candy bar we can buy from the store? Or a toy that we play with for a little while and then grow tired with and leave lying in our toy box, forgotten about?

c. Or do we treat Him like a person? Our friend? A friend who has thoughts and feelings? A friend who has something to say?

d. Do we treat Him like He is Holy? Or do we treat Him like He's something common and ordinary?

e. Do we even give Him much thought?

f. Is He precious to us? Important in our lives?
g. Peter got angry with Simon because Simon had insulted his friend. We don't want to insult Holy Spirit by the way we treat Him.
h. *You may want to take some time to let the children journal or write a letter to Holy Spirit, telling Him how they feel about Him.

Week Eight

The Holy Spirit Speaks

Acts 8:26-39

"For it is not you who speak, but the Spirit of your Father who speaks in you."

Matthew 10:20

I. Review
   a. We've been learning about the Holy Spirit. What have you learned about Him so far?
      i. He lives in us.
      ii. He leads us.
      iii. He strengthens us in our inner man.
      iv. He teaches us about Jesus.
      v. He reminds us of Jesus' words.
      vi. He fills His people. When His people are filled with the Holy Spirit, they have supernatural boldness that they didn't have before.
      vii. He can't be bought because he is a person.
   b. Today we're going to learn how the Holy Spirit speaks.

II. God Speaks to Phillip
   a. Phillip was an apostle of the Lord. This story takes place after what we learned about last week.
   b. Acts 8:26-28- Now an angel of the Lord spoke to Philip, saying, "Arise and go toward the south along the road which goes down from Jerusalem to Gaza." This is desert. 27 So he arose and went. And behold, a man of Ethiopia, a eunuch of great authority under Candace the queen of the Ethiopians, who had charge of all her treasury, and had come to Jerusalem to worship, 28 was returning. And sitting in his chariot, he was reading Isaiah the prophet.
   c. God sent an angel to talk to him. Angels are legit. They are God's messengers. They are all throughout the Bible and people still see angels today. The angel told Phillip to go south along a certain road.
   d. The angel didn't tell Phillip why he wanted him to go south on that road. Phillip probably didn't really know what he was looking for as he followed those instructions.
   e. What did Phillip see as he obeyed God's instructions that were given by the angel?
   f. Phillip saw a very important person from Ethiopia. He worked for the queen there and he was very important in her kingdom.
   g. It says that the Ethiopian was going to Jerusalem to worship. What was he? (He was a Jew.)
   h. Acts 8:29 - Then the Spirit said to Philip, "Go near and overtake this chariot."

i. God then spoke to Phillip through the Holy Spirit. The Holy Spirit told Phillip to run and catch up with the chariot.
j. The Bible doesn't say exactly how Phillip heard the Holy Spirit's voice, but it is likely that the Holy Spirit talked to Phillip much in the same way that He talks to us. This was probably not an audible voice that Phillip could hear with his ears. It wasn't a vision, a dream or an angel. Phillip probably just heard the Holy Spirit whisper these instructions to his heart.

k. Acts 8:30-38- So Philip ran to him, and heard him reading the prophet Isaiah, and said, "Do you understand what you are reading?" 31 And he said, "How can I, unless someone guides me?" And he asked Philip to come up and sit with him. 32 The place in the Scripture which he read was this:

"He was led as a sheep to the slaughter; And as a lamb before its shearer is silent, So He opened not His mouth. 33 In His humiliation His justice was taken away, And who will declare His generation? For His life is taken from the earth."

34 So the eunuch answered Philip and said, "I ask you, of whom does the prophet say this, of himself or of some other man?" 35 Then Philip opened his mouth, and beginning at this Scripture, preached Jesus to him. 36 Now as they went down the road, they came to some water. And the eunuch said, "See, here is water. What hinders me from being baptized?"

37 Then Philip said, "If you believe with all your heart, you may." And he answered and said, "I believe that Jesus Christ is the Son of God." 38 So he commanded the chariot to stand still. And both Philip and the eunuch went down into the water, and he baptized him.

l. The Ethiopian was reading Isaiah and didn't understand it.
m. We've learned how the Holy Spirit is our Helper to help us understand the Scriptures. That means that people who don't have the Holy Spirit can read the Bible and not have a clue what it means. They don't have the Helper inside of them giving them understanding. That's why the Holy Spirit send Phillip to him.
n. Phillip understood the Scriptures. Phillip had the Holy Spirit on the inside of him. So, Phillip was able to explain what they meant. Phillip showed the Ethiopian how Isaiah was talking about Jesus.
o. The Ethiopian was saved and baptized that very day.

p. So, what was all of this for? Why did God send an angel to tell Phillip to go down that road and why did the Holy Spirit tell him to catch up to the chariot?
q. God set up this divine appointment to bring this Ethiopian into His Kingdom. We don't know for sure what happened with this man, but it's very possible that many other people got saved because of this encounter. This man was very influential in his country. If he shared Jesus with others, there would have been a huge opportunity for many others to believe in Jesus as well.

III. The Holy Spirit speaks

a. The Holy Spirit has a lot to say and we can gain a lot of wisdom from Him if we are willing to listen to Him and if we learn how to listen to Him.
b. Mostly it's about paying attention. If Phillip had been distracted with playing a game on his iPhone, he might have missed what the Holy Spirit was saying to him. Of course they didn't have iPhones back then, but there have always been distractions. Those things aren't bad in themselves. We just have to learn when to put them down and how to pay attention to the Holy Spirit's voice.
c. Ask the Holy Spirit to speak to you and then wait. He wants to speak to you more than you want Him to speak to you!
d. Sometimes Holy Spirit gives very specific instructions. He can tell us to go south on a particular street. He can tell us to turn left instead of right. He can tell us to go somewhere different than we normally go or to talk to someone who we wouldn't normally talk to.
e. If we learn to hear His voice, we can hear those very specific instructions. Those instructions might bring us protection, or they might bring salvation to someone else.
f. Since the Holy Spirit lives inside of us, we can talk with Him every day and learn to hear His voice.
g. *For specific training on how to listen for the voice of the Holy Spirit, see "God Speaks School Age Practical Series".

Week Nine

The Holy Spirit is for All

Acts 10:44-48

"Now the Lord is the Spirit; and where the Spirit of the Lord is, there is liberty."

2 Corinthians 3:17

I. Review
   a. We've been learning about the Holy Spirit. What did we learn last week?
   b. How should we treat the Holy Spirit?
   c. Today we're going to learn who the Holy Spirit is for.

II. Jews and Gentiles
   a. Today we're talking about the story of Cornelius. There was a man named Cornelius who was a military officer for Rome. Back then they thought that only Jewish people could be saved, but Cornelius wasn't Jewish. He was a good man who loved God, gave his money to people who needed it and prayed to God all the time. He loved God but didn't know about Jesus.
   b. One afternoon an angel showed up and talked to him!
   c. Acts 10:3-6- One day at about three in the afternoon he had a vision. He distinctly saw an angel of God, who came to him and said, "Cornelius!"

      4 Cornelius stared at him in fear. "What is it, Lord?" he asked.

      The angel answered, "Your prayers and gifts to the poor have come up as a memorial offering before God. **5** Now send men to Joppa to bring back a man named Simon who is called Peter. **6** He is staying with Simon the tanner, whose house is by the sea."
   d. When the angel left him, he told two of his servants and one of his soldiers what had happened and sent them to Joppa to find Peter.
   e. The next day, Peter was on the roof praying waiting while someone was making him lunch. While he was waiting and praying, he fell into a trance, which is kind of like an intense vision.
   f. Acts 10:11-15- He saw heaven opened and something like a large sheet being let down to earth by its four corners. **12** It contained all kinds of four-footed animals, as well as reptiles and birds. **13** Then a voice told him, "Get up, Peter. Kill and eat."

      14 "Surely not, Lord!" Peter replied. "I have never eaten anything impure or unclean."

      15 The voice spoke to him a second time, "Do not call anything impure that God has made clean."
   g. In the laws the God gave Moses, there were rules about what Jewish people could eat and what they couldn't eat. The animals that Jewish

people were not supposed to eat were called unclean animals. In the vision, God told Peter to eat unclean animals, animals that were against Jewish law to eat.

h. Peter told God no! He told God that He had never eaten anything unclean or impure. Like any good Jew, he followed God's laws as best he could.
i. God told him in the vision "Do not call anything impure that God has made clean."
j. This happened three times and then the sheet was taken up into heaven.
k. While Peter was wondering what the vision meant, the men that Cornelius sent stopped at the gate and called out, asking if Simon Peter was there.
l. Acts 10:19-20- While Peter was still thinking about the vision, the Spirit said to him, "Simon, three[a] men are looking for you. **20** So get up and go downstairs. Do not hesitate to go with them, for I have sent them."
m. Why did the Holy Spirit have to tell Peter not to hesitate to go with the men? Why would Peter might not immediately want to go?
n. Not only were Jewish people supposed to not eat certain things, they were supposed to not hang out with Gentiles (people who were non-Jewish). They were supposed to be set apart as God's chosen people, so they weren't supposed to marry Gentiles and mingle with them because God wanted His people to be different from the world around them. Because of this, Jews didn't even go into Gentiles houses! And Cornelius was a Gentile.
o. Cornelius' men told Peter how an angel showed up to Cornelius and Peter invited them to stay the night. The next day Peter went with them to Cornelius' house where Cornelius had gathered all of his relatives to hear what Peter had to say.
p. Acts 10:28-29- He said to them: "You are well aware that it is against our law for a Jew to associate with or visit a Gentile. But God has shown me that I should not call anyone impure or unclean. **29** So when I was sent for, I came without raising any objection. May I ask why you sent for me?"
q. Cornelius told him what the angel said and then said "So I sent for you immediately, and it was good of you to come. Now we are all here in the presence of God to listen to everything the Lord has commanded you to tell us." (vs. 33)
r. Peter told everyone there about Jesus and how they could receive forgiveness of their sins through His name.
s. Acts 10:44-46- While Peter was still speaking these words, the Holy Spirit came on all who heard the message. **45** The circumcised believers who had come with Peter were astonished that the gift of the Holy Spirit had been poured out even on Gentiles. **46** For they heard them speaking in tongues and praising God.

t. The Holy Spirit was so excited to be poured out on the Gentiles that He couldn't even wait for Peter to finish his sermon. While Peter was still talking, the Holy Spirit came upon everyone who heard the message.
u. The Jewish people had spent their entire lives thinking that because they were God's chosen people that meant that God was only concerned with saving them. Now they saw that the Holy Spirit was being poured out on the Gentiles too. They were surprised and amazed! God must care about everybody He created.
v. Acts 10:47-48- Then Peter said, **47** "Surely no one can stand in the way of their being baptized with water. They have received the Holy Spirit just as we have."**48** So he ordered that they be baptized in the name of Jesus Christ. Then they asked Peter to stay with them for a few days.

III. Who does He not love?

a. Peter loved Jesus very much. They were very close friends. When Jesus went back to heaven, Peter started to develop a close relationship with the Holy Spirit. He loved God. He knew God loved Him. Now God was showing him who else God loved.
b. Most of us are probably Gentiles and in our culture, we don't really understand why it was such a big deal that the Holy Spirit was poured out on the Gentiles. It was a big deal at the time!
c. Today, we can think about how the Holy Spirit is for everyone. Who does He not love? Who does He not want to come and live inside? Who does He not want to fill?
d. Everyone is created by God and the Holy Spirit longs to be poured out on all of His creation. There is no one off limits.
e. What about the poor? Does the Holy Spirit want to be poured out on the poor? Yes! What about the rich? Do you think they are too snobby? Does the Holy Spirit want to be poured out on them? Yes!
f. Who doesn't look like you? Think like you? Act like you? You might think, even in the back of your mind, that the Holy Spirit isn't for them, but it's not true. The Holy Spirit is for everyone. God desires for ALL people to be saved. When they trust Jesus to be their Savior, they can be filled with the Holy Spirit.
g. What about people of different religions? What about Muslims? Buddhists? Atheists? Does the Holy Spirit want to live inside of them too? Yes! Just like an angel showed up to Cornelius, people who don't know Jesus can have angelic encounters and be saved. They can hear the gospel, repent, and be filled with the Holy Spirit!
h. What about those boys and girls at school who are mean? The bullies? Does the Holy Spirit want to fill them up? Yes! God wants to touch their hearts with His love and fill them with the Holy Spirit.
i. Think about the group of people that you think seem the farthest from God right now and pray for them. Pray that they would be saved, and the God would pour out the Holy Spirit on them. The Holy Spirit gives people power to change.

Week Ten

The Holy Spirit Directs

Acts 16:6-10

"Likewise the Spirit also helps in our weaknesses. For we do not know what we should pray for as we ought, but the Spirit Himself makes intercession for us with groanings which cannot be uttered. Now He who searches the hearts knows what the mind of the Spirit is, because He makes intercession for the saints according to the will of God."

Romans 8:26-27

I. Review
   a. Name three things the Holy Spirit does.
   b. Last week we learned about Cornelius and Peter. What did that story show us about the Holy Spirit?
   c. This week we're going to see how the Holy Spirit directs His people.

II. The Holy Spirit directs the apostles
   a. Paul, Silas, and Timothy were apostles who went all over by boat to different churches to encourage and strengthen them.
   b. Acts 16:5- So the churches were strengthened in the faith and grew daily in numbers.
   c. As they were traveling, the Holy Spirit directed them. We talked before about how the Holy Spirit led Simeon to the temple at just the right time so that He could meet the Messiah. In this story, we see the Holy Spirit leading in a different way.
   d. Acts 16:6- Paul and his companions traveled throughout the region of Phrygia and Galatia, having been kept by the Holy Spirit from preaching the word in the province of Asia. (*Show map)
   e. Did you catch that? The Holy Spirit stopped them from preaching the gospel in Asia. Why would the Holy Spirit do that? Doesn't He want everyone everywhere to know about Jesus? Why didn't He want those apostles to preach the gospel in Asia?
   f. Acts 16:7-8- [7] When they came to the border of Mysia, they tried to enter Bithynia, but the Spirit of Jesus would not allow them to. [8] So they passed by Mysia and went down to Troas. (*Show map)
   g. "The Spirit of Jesus" is just another way of saying The Holy Spirit. Here again the apostles tried to go one way, to Bithynia, but the Holy Spirit put out a big red stop sign. He wasn't having it.
   h. What do you think the apostles were thinking and feeling at this point? It seems like everywhere they try to go, the Holy Spirit says "no". And it doesn't seem like He tells them why! That could be frustrating. It would be very frustrating if you didn't know the Holy Spirit well enough to trust that He always has a very good reason for saying no.
   i. Acts 16:9-10- During the night Paul had a vision of a man of Macedonia standing and begging him, "Come over to Macedonia and help us." [10] After Paul had seen the vision, we got ready at once to leave for Macedonia, concluding that God had called us to preach the gospel to them.

j. Finally, they are given an explanation. The Holy Spirit said no to Asia and no to Bithynia because it was on His heart for the apostles to go to Macedonia instead.
k. The people of Macedonia really needed to hear the gospel and they were ready to hear it!
l. What would have happened if the apostles wouldn't have listened to the Holy Spirit and instead would have went to Asia anyway? Do you think they would have seen much fruit in Asia? (Much fruit means many people getting saved, healed, and delivered.)
m. What would have happened to the people in Macedonia if the apostles wouldn't have listened to the Holy Spirit and instead would have went to Bithynia?
n. The Holy Spirit knew where the harvest would be ripe. He knew where people were ready for Him. He knew the best place for the apostles to go. If the apostles were to go anywhere else, they might still have seen God do great things because God is still God no matter what. However, they might not have had nearly as much impact as they could have had and as they longed to have.

III. When a door closes

a. No one likes to be told no, unless maybe they are asking if they have to eat their broccoli!
b. When we have something we are planning to do, it can be hard when that door closes. When can feel frustrated if we don't understand why.
c. However, part of learning to be led by the Holy Spirit is learning to hear and respect when He is saying no to something. He always, 100% of the time has a good reason.
d. Sometimes you parents might say no to something you want and maybe their reason isn't 100% the best. Maybe they are just tired at that moment and don't want to deal with what you are asking them to do. But when the Holy Spirit says no, it's always, 100% for the best. It's for your best and for the best of whoever else is involved.
e. We know that the Holy Spirit is the Spirit of wisdom and revelation. That means He's beyond smart. He is Wisdom itself! He never makes a mistake. He never makes a wrong move. We never need to question whether His decisions are the right ones.
f. If the Holy Spirit is saying no to something, it's only because He's saying yes to something else. He loves to say yes! He loves to say yes to God's plans and purposes on the earth. He loves to say yes to His Kingdom invading earth. He loves to say yes to your joy. If you hear Him saying no to something, go ahead and ask Him what He is saying yes to. Like the apostles, you might have to wait a little while for the answer but it will be worth it.

IV. Pay attention

a. The Holy Spirit didn't really direct the apostles with a big red stop sign. He didn't write the word "NO!" in the sky.

b. The Bible doesn't say how the Holy Spirit prevented them from going to Asia or Bithynia, but it was probably with that still small voice spoken to their hearts.
c. That means the apostles had to have been paying attention. They had to have been asking the Holy Spirit what He wanted and listening for the answer. They had to have hearts that were sensitive to what the Holy Spirit was doing.
d. If they had been distracted, busy playing with their Xbox and stuffing their faces with Cheetos, they could have missed what the Holy Spirit was saying.
e. That's not to say that video games and those things are all bad, but if we want to be directed by the Holy Spirit, we have to position our hearts to hear from Him. We have to take some time to step away from all of the distractions and talk to Him and ask Him what's on His mind.
f. The Holy Spirit knows the Father's heart. He can tell us what God wants us to do. We can learn to let Him direct us. When we let Him direct us, God can use us in powerful ways!

Week Eleven

The Holy Spirit Dwells in Us!

1 Cor. 6:19

"The Spirit Himself bears witness with our spirit that we are children of God."

Romans 8:16

I. Review
  a. This is our last week learning about the Holy Spirit. Let's talk about what you've learned so far? What does the Holy Spirit do?
    i. Leads
    ii. Strengthens
    iii. Teaches
    iv. Reminds
    v. Fills
    vi. Speaks
    vii. Directs
  b. Where does the Holy Spirit live?
  c. Who is the Holy Spirit for?
  d. Who does the Holy Spirit love to talk about?
  e. What is the sword of the Spirit (The Holy Spirit's weapon)?
  f. We've already learned about how the Holy Spirit lives inside of those who believe in Jesus. Today we're going to go into more detail about what that means.

II. His Temple
  a. 1 Corinthians 6:19-20- Do you not know that your bodies are temples of the Holy Spirit, who is in you, whom you have received from God? You are not your own; **20** you were bought at a price. Therefore honor God with your bodies."
  b. The Bible says that our bodies are the temple of the Holy Spirit. What is a temple? (show picture)
  c. The temple in the Old Testament was God's house. At first, God told Moses to build him a tabernacle, which was a tent. The Ark of the Covenant was where God's presence rested, and that Ark was kept in the tabernacle.
  d. When David was king, he took made a different tabernacle. He took that Ark that Moses had kept hidden in the Holy of Holies and brought it right out into the open. He had people worship around God's presence.
  e. After the Tabernacle of David, David's son Solomon built a magnificent building to be God's house. David didn't build the temple, but he prepared for it. David was sad that he lived in this fancy palace, but God was dwelling in a tent. So, David set out to get a bunch of gold, silver, and bronze together so that his son Solomon could build a beautiful temple for God.
  f. Solomon went to work overseeing the building of the temple. He made sure everything was made with excellence because he wanted God to have the best.

g. When the temple was finished, Solomon dedicated it to God and prayed to Him.
h. Do you know what happened when he was done?
i. 2 Chronicles 7:1-3- When Solomon finished praying, fire came down from heaven and consumed the burnt offering and the sacrifices, and the glory of the LORD filled the temple. 2 The priests could not enter the temple of the LORD because the glory of the LORD filled it. 3 When all the Israelites saw the fire coming down and the glory of the LORD above the temple, they knelt on the pavement with their faces to the ground, and they worshiped and gave thanks to the LORD, saying,

"He is good;
his love endures forever."

j. When Solomon finished dedicated the temple, God showed up! Fire came down from heaven and His glory filled the temple. The glory of God was so thick, the priests couldn't even get in the door! It was like a thick cloud of glory.
k. If we love and follow Jesus, we are God's temple. The Holy Spirit comes and fills us like God's glory filled Solomon's temple.
l. Even though we still do everyday ordinary things, those normal things become holy things when we do them for God in partnership with the Holy Spirit inside of us.

III. A special place

a. If you are a follower of Jesus, you have God on the inside of you! God! The very God who created the universe. The same God who parted the Red Sea for the Israelites when they were leaving Egypt lives inside you. The same God who heals every kind of sickness and disease lives inside you. Nothing is impossible for Him. Nothing is too hard. And He lives IN YOU!
b. Do you remember the story of the burning bush? Moses saw a bush that was on fire but didn't burn up. We are like that burning bush. We have the Holy Spirit – that holy flame of Love- burning on the inside of us and yet we don't burn up! It's amazing!
c. David and Solomon worked to make sure the temple was magnificent and full of the finest gold and workmanship. They knew that it wouldn't be right for such a holy God to live in a shack.
d. God has chosen to live inside of you. Don't you think that places value on you? Don't you think that makes you special? Do you think God would want to live inside someone that He thought was ugly or insignificant? Would God want to live inside someone He thought was stupid or boring? No!
e. God chose to live inside human beings because He loves people! He has placed His love on you. It's like He couldn't get enough of you, so He just had to move in!

IV. The Spirit of Adoption

a. Our memory verse today tells us that the Holy Spirit reminds us that we are children of God.
b. Romans 8:16- The Spirit Himself bears witness with our spirit that we are children of God.
c. Whenever we feel like we are not very special, the Holy Spirit can help us to know that we are God's own children and that He loves us.
d. We've talked about how much the Holy Spirit loves to talk about Jesus. Now we see that the Holy Spirit loves to talk to us about the Father as well. He loves to remind us that the Father is OUR Father, and that we are His children. The Holy Spirit loves to remind us that we have been brought into the family of God.
e. Romans 8:15- For you did not receive the spirit of bondage again to fear, but you received the Spirit of adoption by whom we cry out, "Abba, Father."
f. Another name for the Holy Spirit is the Spirit of adoption. He shows us that we have been adopted into God's family and that we are children of God. We come to the Father through the Holy Spirit.
g. Orphans are children that have been left by their father and mother, either because their parents have died, because of hard circumstances, or because their parents chose to leave. We are not orphans. We are children of God and we know that we are in God's family because the Holy Spirit never leaves. He lives inside of us. He never goes away.
h. If you are a follower of Jesus, the Holy Spirit is always with you. He can't be any more with you than He already is. However, you can pray that you recognize His presence and that you feel His presence on your heart. When we pray for the Holy Spirit to "fill us up", we are praying to be able to be aware of His presence and live connected to Him.
i. The Holy Spirit is an amazing gift to us from the Father. He loves to give good gifts to His children and the Holy Spirit is the best gift of all!

Family Connection

Week One

Car Talk

Conversation starters for the ride home

1. Who is the Holy Spirit?
2. Has the Holy Spirit always been alive?
3. Before Jesus came, what did the Holy Spirit do?
4. Where does the Holy Spirit live now?

Prayer Jump Start

Feel free to use this to jump start a prayer of your own to God.

Holy Spirit, thank You for living inside of me. Reveal Yourself to me.

Memory Verse

"And I will pray the Father, and He will give you another Helper, that He may abide with you forever— the Spirit of truth, whom the world cannot receive, because it neither sees Him nor knows Him; but you know Him, for He dwells with you and will be in you. I will not leave you orphans; I will come to you." John 14:16-18

Just For Fun

V	K	O	Z	V	H	W	F	K	N	S	Z	W	Q	P
R	X	I	E	G	T	L	M	Y	P	O	P	A	B	R
N	Z	W	I	O	U	U	E	P	Y	K	S	N	V	I
L	B	I	Q	C	R	A	S	R	B	T	H	R	T	H
L	H	X	T	M	T	S	H	O	S	Z	W	L	E	X
T	L	I	N	D	F	G	F	P	D	W	F	I	S	P
B	E	F	A	Z	O	Q	I	H	C	R	V	V	F	L
B	O	V	L	N	T	L	X	E	N	K	R	E	C	O
F	I	T	L	P	I	V	W	S	T	E	G	S	O	P
D	Q	E	W	E	R	Y	O	Y	P	G	Z	I	M	W
V	I	Z	F	A	I	K	H	L	E	V	F	N	E	G
G	Z	V	R	P	P	L	E	F	J	G	G	S	U	K
Y	C	H	Z	T	S	H	P	J	I	E	C	I	P	T
E	M	P	O	W	E	R	S	T	F	G	U	D	O	L
D	U	Q	G	O	D	U	O	I	Q	Z	T	E	N	U

COME UPON
DAVID
EMPOWERS
GOD
HELPER
LIVES INSIDE
PERSON
PROPHESY
SAUL
SPIRIT OF TRUTH

What do each of these words have to do with today's lesson?

Going Deeper

Read Numbers 27:18, Judges 3:10, and Judges 6:34. Who did the Holy Spirit come upon in those verses and why?

Family Connection

Week Two

Car Talk

Conversation starters for the ride home

1. Why were Joseph and Mary at the temple?
2. How did Simeon know to go to the temple?
3. How did Simeon know that the baby Jesus was the Messiah?
4. What did Simeon do when he saw baby Jesus?
5. Can we be led by the Holy Spirit too?

Prayer Jump Start

Feel free to use this to jump start a prayer of your own to God.

Holy Spirit, help me to pay attention to you. Lead me and guide me.

Memory Verse

"But God has revealed them to us through His Spirit. For the Spirit searches all things, yes, the deep things of God. For what man knows the things of a man except the spirit of the man which is in him? Even so no one knows the things of God except the Spirit of God." 1 Corinthians 2:10-11

Just For Fun

E	L	T	T	Q	Z	S	W	H	Y	M	H	B	X	H
S	L	E	T	Y	G	I	Y	G	V	O	O	D	P	A
K	H	P	A	Y	M	M	F	Z	T	N	L	T	M	I
F	T	Q	M	D	F	E	Y	Z	C	Z	Y	T	N	S
N	Q	Z	J	E	S	O	R	M	Y	H	S	Q	L	S
V	O	K	V	V	T	N	K	P	E	J	P	K	H	E
K	S	I	L	F	Y	D	B	R	T	G	I	D	F	M
A	Z	N	R	H	O	A	S	O	R	C	R	N	L	I
H	P	M	V	K	Y	R	X	O	M	H	I	M	S	R
C	G	H	K	L	J	S	I	C	D	O	T	L	F	Z
A	J	R	A	U	T	O	A	S	E	D	I	U	G	W
W	Y	J	F	Z	J	V	S	M	R	B	W	G	X	Z
P	R	O	P	H	E	S	Y	E	A	K	Z	X	O	C
C	Q	V	H	Q	S	Q	E	N	P	R	Q	G	J	F
S	U	S	E	J	C	N	W	Y	L	H	Y	C	I	B

GUIDES
HOLY SPIRIT
JESUS
JOSEPH
LEADS
MARY
MESSIAH
PROPHESY
SIMEON
TEMPLE

What do each of these words have to do with today's lesson?

Going Deeper

Read in Luke 2:36-38 about someone else who was in the temple. The Bible doesn't say specifically that she was led by the Holy Spirit, but it gives us a pretty good clue that she was. How can we tell?

Family Connection

Week Three

Car Talk

Conversation starters for the ride home

1. Where did the Holy Spirit lead Jesus? Why?
2. What did the devil try to do? Did it work?
3. What did Jesus use to fight the devil?
4. What did the Holy Spirit do?

Prayer Jump Start

Feel free to use this to jump start a prayer of your own to God.

Holy Spirit, strengthen me with might. Teach me how to use the sword of the Spirit.

Memory Verse

"That He would grant you, according to the riches of his glory to be strengthened with might by His Spirit in the inner man." Ephesians 3:16

Just For Fun

F	F	T	L	N	D	K	F	A	M	J	T	S	W	R
S	S	E	N	R	E	D	L	I	W	E	U	B	H	U
S	J	G	A	T	Y	C	W	L	M	S	P	E	H	W
S	T	E	R	U	D	P	R	P	E	E	M	W	V	T
Y	C	R	C	M	D	H	T	J	I	A	N	D	G	V
F	X	X	E	L	G	E	V	N	T	W	B	D	F	V
N	Z	L	E	N	D	D	R	P	N	J	A	Q	K	Z
L	M	A	R	T	G	D	O	G	F	O	D	R	O	W
W	D	W	H	L	I	T	T	E	A	N	L	F	O	E
Z	K	G	Z	H	Y	E	H	Y	Q	G	B	C	C	F
O	I	U	P	M	W	S	S	E	U	E	C	N	M	X
M	B	Q	L	M	C	G	K	B	N	A	Z	L	Y	V
G	K	P	J	S	H	Q	O	E	Z	S	M	M	I	B
N	E	T	T	I	R	W	S	I	T	I	H	K	L	E
R	G	C	Y	J	N	O	W	X	I	F	C	W	U	A

IT IS WRITTEN
JESUS
LEAD
MIGHT
RHEMA
STRENGTHENS
TEMPTED
WILDERNESS
WORD OF GOD

What do each of these words have to do with today's lesson?

Going Deeper

Read about the armor of God in Ephesians 6:10-18. What are the other pieces of armor? Where else in this passage is the Holy Spirit mentioned?

Family Connection
Week Four

Car Talk

Conversation starters for the ride home

1. What did Jesus tell His disciples not to be afraid to do?
2. Who did God send to help His disciples tell others about Jesus?
3. What job is the Holy Spirit really good at?
4. How did the Holy Spirit help Paul?
5. Who does the Holy Spirit love to talk about?

Prayer Jump Start

Feel free to use this to jump start a prayer of your own to God.

Holy Spirit, teach me what You want me to know.

Memory Verse

"For the Holy Spirit will teach you in that very hour what you ought to say." Luke 12:12

Just For Fun 

U	Y	J	K	E	V	L	X	Z	S	Y	D	D	N	I
N	N	A	W	I	R	A	C	U	I	G	Q	L	I	I
L	O	D	Y	Z	D	U	S	X	C	H	E	I	A	D
N	U	M	E	V	S	E	T	W	Q	S	I	U	G	K
I	W	K	Y	R	J	H	Q	P	N	C	W	B	A	X
T	M	X	N	X	S	M	E	S	I	Z	I	E	E	N
R	E	M	I	N	D	T	E	L	J	R	C	R	S	W
R	G	T	F	B	Z	L	A	H	P	V	C	V	I	B
V	Y	N	F	E	P	S	Y	N	U	E	C	S	R	I
X	O	Y	E	I	N	Q	A	H	D	F	R	E	Q	L
T	I	B	C	L	R	X	M	C	V	I	V	E	W	N
L	S	S	I	A	P	S	B	A	W	F	N	J	B	N
P	I	L	J	A	S	M	E	E	Z	Z	Z	G	F	N
D	O	X	W	S	Y	Y	E	T	N	T	A	N	Q	X
E	M	Q	O	O	O	C	L	T	I	K	A	L	T	L

DISCIPLES
HELPER
JESUS
REBUILD
REMIND
RISEAGAIN
SCRIPTURE
TEACH
TEMPLE
UNDERSTANDING

What do each of these words have to do with today's lesson?

Going Deeper

Read Paul's entire address to King Agrippa in Acts 25. Highlight the parts that stick out to you the most. Why do you think King Agrippa was moved?

Family Connection Week Five

Car Talk

Conversation starters for the ride home

1. What is the Holy Spirit called? Why?
2. What did Jesus tell the disciples the Holy Spirit would do for them?
3. What did the Holy Spirit remind the disciples of in John 2?
4. How can the Holy Spirit help us?

Prayer Jump Start

Feel free to use this to jump start a prayer of your own to God.

Holy Spirit, thank you for being the Helper. Help me to understand the Scriptures. Give me revelation.

Memory Verse

"But the Helper, the Holy Spirit, whom the Father will send in My name, He will teach you all things, and bring to your remembrance all things that I said to you." John 14:26

Just For Fun

U	Y	J	K	E	V	L	X	Z	S	Y	D	D	N	I
N	N	A	W	I	R	A	C	U	I	G	Q	L	I	I
L	O	D	Y	Z	D	U	S	X	C	H	E	I	A	D
N	U	M	E	V	S	E	T	W	Q	S	I	U	G	K
I	W	K	Y	R	J	H	Q	P	N	C	W	B	A	X
T	M	X	N	X	S	M	E	S	I	Z	I	E	E	N
R	E	M	I	N	D	T	E	L	J	R	C	R	S	W
R	G	T	F	B	Z	L	A	H	P	V	C	V	I	B
V	Y	N	F	E	P	S	Y	N	U	E	C	S	R	I
X	O	Y	E	I	N	Q	A	H	D	F	R	E	Q	L
T	I	B	C	L	R	X	M	C	V	I	V	E	W	N
L	S	S	I	A	P	S	B	A	W	F	N	J	B	N
P	I	L	J	A	S	M	E	E	Z	Z	Z	G	F	N
D	O	X	W	S	Y	Y	E	T	N	T	A	N	Q	X
E	M	Q	O	O	O	C	L	T	I	K	A	L	T	L

DISCIPLES
HELPER
JESUS
REBUILD
REMIND
RISE AGAIN
SCRIPTURE
TEACH
TEMPLE
UNDERSTANDING

What do each of these words have to do with today's lesson?

Going Deeper

Read John 12:12-16. What did the Holy Spirit remind the disciples of and teach them about in that passage?

Family Connection

Week Six

Car Talk

Conversation starters for the ride home

1. What did Jesus promise His disciples before He died and came back to life?
2. What did the Holy Spirit sound like when He came?
3. What did the Holy Spirit look like when He came?
4. What did the Holy Spirit do? (fill them)
5. What did they do when they were full of the Holy Spirit?

Prayer Jump Start

Feel free to use this to jump start a prayer of your own to God.

Holy Spirit, fill me up!

Memory Verse

"All of them were filled with the Holy Spirit and began to speak in other tongues as the Spirit enabled them." Acts 2:4

Just For Fun

Z	Q	I	T	T	Y	C	U	D	B	X	O	W	P	M
Q	Z	W	U	Y	I	R	E	E	L	C	A	R	O	O
H	C	R	I	T	S	N	S	V	Z	I	O	C	Q	J
L	B	E	N	L	S	I	G	A	T	M	K	T	N	W
L	Z	T	V	G	S	O	D	S	I	E	Q	L	R	V
B	W	E	T	B	F	Y	C	S	D	Y	C	M	S	L
W	M	P	C	J	V	Q	E	E	A	U	H	I	E	Y
K	R	Q	Q	Q	H	D	O	Y	T	K	D	S	U	E
W	N	Q	O	R	L	T	N	C	R	N	A	B	G	Q
R	U	S	H	I	N	G	W	I	N	D	E	U	N	R
F	S	Y	K	F	Y	G	R	O	W	P	C	P	O	T
X	X	J	U	I	L	I	D	S	J	X	P	Z	T	X
M	N	G	Z	R	X	U	C	Q	N	O	M	R	E	S
L	X	D	Z	E	M	V	G	Z	P	J	I	X	O	I
Z	T	A	G	P	A	A	G	V	S	A	H	Z	R	B

FIRE
MOCKED
PENTECOST
PETER
PROMISE
RUSHING WIND
SAVED
SERMON
TONGUES
WAIT

What do each of these words have to do with today's lesson?

Going Deeper

Read Peter's sermon in Acts 2:14-39. How did the Holy Spirit help him to know what to speak?

Family Connection
Week Seven

Car Talk

Conversation starters for the ride home

1. What did Phillip do in Samaria?
2. Who listened to him and believed in Jesus?
3. What happened when Peter and John prayed for people?
4. What did Simon do?
5. What did Peter say? Why?

Prayer Jump Start

Feel free to use this to jump start a prayer of your own to God.

Holy Spirit, I love You. Help me to treat You as You ought to be treated.

Memory Verse

"It is the Spirit who gives life; the flesh profits nothing. The words that I speak to you are spirit, and they are life." John 6:63

Just For Fun

P	N	H	O	J	P	Q	N	S	S	Q	S	U	K	R
V	O	E	R	H	C	O	D	D	A	F	Z	I	F	E
Z	U	U	I	L	M	E	R	N	M	F	A	K	P	P
F	J	L	R	I	P	E	Q	A	A	Q	R	B	J	E
I	I	K	S	E	W	B	M	H	R	F	I	O	D	N
P	W	T	L	O	D	E	W	Y	I	P	O	K	W	T
X	D	I	P	J	T	O	P	A	A	M	O	N	E	Y
Z	J	E	N	C	R	J	U	L	R	N	Y	J	S	T
O	Q	R	E	T	E	P	Q	T	Z	E	G	X	C	B
Z	Q	F	D	A	Z	B	Y	N	X	H	Z	W	Z	D
H	Q	W	E	H	J	N	U	W	G	Z	E	T	D	J
H	W	S	A	K	M	E	Z	T	B	X	S	H	R	L
Y	Z	P	Y	B	C	A	L	K	X	I	S	B	L	G
M	U	X	M	H	C	U	O	K	A	O	X	J	K	U
D	A	G	Z	U	X	Q	C	V	P	H	H	C	O	H

JOHN
LAY HANDS
MONEY
PETER
PHILIP
POURED OUT
POWER
REPENT
SAMARIA
SIMON

What do each of these words have to do with today's lesson?

Going Deeper

Read Ephesians 4:30. How does this verse show how the Holy Spirit is a person even though He is fully God.

Family Connection

Week Eight

Car Talk

Conversation starters for the ride home

1. What did the Holy Spirit say to Phillip?
2. Why couldn't the Ethiopian understand what he was reading?
3. Why could Phillip understand it?
4. What happened to the Ethiopian?
5. Does the Holy Spirit still speak today?

Prayer Jump Start

Feel free to use this to jump start a prayer of your own to God.

Holy Spirit, speak to me. Teach me how to listen to your voice. Help me to pay attention to You.

Memory Verse

"For it is not you who speak, but the Spirit of your Father who speaks in you."
Matthew 10:20

Just For Fun

P	I	L	D	U	K	R	Z	B	K	B	N	J	C	V
I	N	I	M	E	D	Y	A	V	Y	E	S	Y	A	N
X	E	R	X	F	V	P	M	I	F	Z	I	N	T	K
G	F	T	T	E	T	A	C	H	N	S	O	S	C	L
T	D	J	H	I	X	G	S	U	E	I	T	N	H	G
W	T	O	Z	I	O	D	R	T	T	L	I	T	U	L
D	H	E	W	J	O	Q	E	N	P	H	O	K	P	Z
I	D	M	C	Y	N	P	E	P	I	L	L	I	H	P
W	F	W	V	V	C	T	I	G	Z	T	B	I	C	L
J	Q	X	F	N	T	Y	X	A	P	P	H	F	X	C
P	A	L	T	A	Z	D	R	U	N	B	T	S	J	O
P	C	J	Y	I	I	Y	E	L	Y	Y	A	K	Q	E
L	B	A	C	R	W	K	M	L	R	P	I	Y	J	L
F	P	E	X	P	L	A	I	N	S	K	A	E	P	S
G	Z	D	T	D	X	X	E	Y	Q	K	Q	V	G	Z

BAPTIZED
CATCH UP
ETHIOPIAN
EXPLAIN
PAY ATTENTION
PHILLIP
RUN
SAVED
SPEAKS

What do each of these words have to do with today's lesson?

Going Deeper

Read the rest of the story in Acts 8:39-40. What did the Holy Spirit do to Phillip? Did you have any idea that the Holy Spirit could do that?

Family Connection
Week Nine

Car Talk

Conversation starters for the ride home

1. Who was Cornelius?
2. What did Peter do?
3. What happened when Peter told Cornelius and his household about Jesus?
4. What did Peter know then? (that the Holy Spirit is for everybody!)

Prayer Jump Start

Feel free to use this to jump start a prayer of your own to God.

Holy Spirit, thank You that You love everyone and that You want to be poured out on all people. Show me who You would like me to pray for, that they might be saved and filled with You.

Memory Verse

"Now the Lord is the Spirit; and where the Spirit of the Lord is, there is liberty."
2 Corinthians 3:17

Just For Fun

C	T	P	A	S	T	L	A	D	Q	B	A	B	M	P
R	D	V	Y	E	U	Q	J	A	C	N	I	A	E	Y
J	L	G	E	Z	Q	I	U	Y	G	V	M	G	D	T
W	N	H	K	W	A	Z	L	E	I	M	K	O	M	R
I	S	H	S	U	V	T	L	E	R	Y	B	P	B	A
P	O	U	R	E	D	O	U	T	N	Y	H	X	L	N
R	G	O	J	V	A	E	I	C	R	R	P	I	M	C
G	E	E	Q	A	G	O	B	E	Y	Y	O	E	F	E
U	W	T	V	M	R	G	V	D	T	R	E	C	Q	S
S	Q	B	E	E	Y	E	D	E	V	A	S	T	R	P
Y	E	F	V	P	Y	G	G	K	M	Y	I	Z	T	S
Q	F	Q	M	B	Z	P	Y	C	V	F	Y	S	K	M
K	S	N	S	E	L	I	T	N	E	G	B	G	W	G
S	T	Z	I	M	Y	N	S	I	J	F	Q	W	I	A
N	Q	W	G	Q	C	K	F	M	R	M	S	W	A	W

ANGEL
CORNELIUS
EVERYBODY
GENTILES
JEWS
PETER
POURED OUT
SAVED
SHEET
TRANCE

What do each of these words have to do with today's lesson?

Going Deeper

Read Peter's whole sermon in Acts 10:34-43. Who did Peter say Jesus was anointed with in verse 38? What did that enable Him to do?

Family Connection

Week Ten

Car Talk

Conversation starters for the ride home

1. What were Paul, Silas and Timothy doing?
2. What did the Holy Spirit do?
3. What did Paul see in a vision?
4. Where did they end up going?

Prayer Jump Start

Feel free to use this to jump start a prayer of your own to God.

Holy Spirit, I want to be directed by you. Show me what You are saying yes to right now.

Memory Verse

"Likewise the Spirit also helps in our weaknesses. For we do not know what we should pray for as we ought, but the Spirit Himself makes intercession for us with groanings which cannot be uttered. Now He who searches the hearts knows what the mind of the Spirit is, because He makes intercession for the saints according to the will of God." Romans 8:26-27

Just For Fun

R	L	V	N	N	T	X	B	L	Y	K	R	U	Y	M
P	O	V	U	I	O	I	T	P	E	N	C	K	J	E
P	U	O	U	S	T	Y	S	H	V	N	D	W	Z	V
Z	D	R	D	H	E	W	D	K	N	O	I	S	I	V
H	F	L	Y	D	Q	L	K	W	I	O	I	L	H	M
Y	T	N	P	E	E	F	T	H	J	Z	O	E	A	X
I	I	Z	Z	T	X	S	C	S	W	G	X	P	U	E
A	A	I	S	A	S	V	O	L	O	G	L	S	A	C
A	G	H	F	S	F	Y	I	L	S	P	L	O	P	I
B	P	W	N	U	B	X	L	U	C	R	A	G	I	O
U	X	E	N	P	V	Q	B	S	P	H	E	X	H	L
L	M	T	U	M	J	T	G	U	O	Q	G	B	F	U
A	I	N	O	D	E	C	A	M	P	A	U	L	W	E
D	I	R	E	C	T	S	G	T	V	Z	Z	J	Y	C
J	E	U	Z	X	H	M	E	R	D	Y	B	L	U	G

APOSTLES
ASIA
BITHYNIA
CLOSED DOOR
DIRECTS
FRUIT
GOSPEL
MACEDONIA
PAUL
VISION

What do each of these words have to do with today's lesson?

Going Deeper

Read Acts 16:13-15. What happened when the apostles got to Macedonia? Who came to know Jesus there? Have you heard the story from Acts 16:33-40? That happened in Macedonia as well!

Family Connection

Week Eleven

Car Talk

Conversation starters for the ride home

1. What is a temple?
2. What is the Holy Spirit's temple?
3. What is another name for the Holy Spirit?
4. What does the Holy Spirit show us?

Prayer Jump Start

Feel free to use this to jump start a prayer of your own to God.

Holy Spirit, thank you for living inside of me. Help me to be aware of Your presence.

Memory Verse

"The Spirit Himself bears witness with our spirit that we are children of God." Romans 8:16

Just For Fun

N	E	G	E	S	S	X	S	C	T	U	N	G	G	H
N	O	H	L	P	M	W	G	E	Z	O	A	C	X	D
B	O	I	I	O	L	A	T	F	M	Y	D	O	B	B
R	U	R	T	L	R	I	Q	O	K	L	C	B	P	N
I	I	R	B	P	P	Y	L	B	F	U	Y	A	W	C
T	N	T	N	N	O	O	G	J	W	F	Q	L	T	S
P	S	S	G	I	S	D	G	Z	Q	I	E	R	O	Q
G	D	S	I	U	N	V	A	G	A	T	J	D	H	H
X	R	O	K	D	R	G	X	T	H	U	V	F	R	F
X	I	M	U	R	E	E	B	D	Y	A	E	X	E	H
U	Q	K	O	G	Q	K	H	U	R	E	L	R	D	O
J	O	C	D	M	G	R	M	T	S	B	P	F	U	M
B	Q	L	B	O	D	L	E	S	A	H	M	V	K	M
O	J	V	L	E	Q	U	T	E	W	F	E	V	A	M
T	Z	D	F	K	X	Z	C	E	F	K	T	C	R	R

ADOPTION
BEAUTIFUL
BODY
BURNING BUSH
FATHER
GLORY
GOLD
HOLY
INSIDE
SOLOMON
SPIRIT
TEMPLE

What do each of these words have to do with today's lesson?

Going Deeper

Read 2 Chronicles 3. What precious materials were used to build Solomon's temple? What does that tell us about who God is? What does that tell us about who we are?

Looking for more?
Try another curriculum from Equipping the Children.

School Age Curricula

GOD SPEAKS STORY SERIES* & GOD SPEAKS PRACTICAL SERIES
GOD HEALS STORY SERIES* & GOD HEALS PRACTICAL SERIES
GOD LISTENS STORY SERIES* & GOD LISTENS PRACTICAL SERIES
GOD PROVIDES STORY SERIES* & GOD PROVIDES PRACTICAL SERIES
I AM*
THE FATHER*
THE HOLY SPIRIT*
THE TRINITY*
THE SEED*
THE SAVIOR*
THE LION*
THE LAMB*
THE PARABLES*

***Also available as Early Childhood curricula.**

Printed in Great Britain
by Amazon

23730372R00033